What is LIGHT?

First published in 2018 by Wayland
Copyright © Hodder and Stoughton 2018

Wayland
Carmelite House
50 Victoria Embankment
London EC4Y 0DZ

Managing editor: Victoria Brooker
Creative design: Paul Cherrill

ISBN: 978 1 5263 0660 9

Printed in China

FSC
www.fsc.org

MIX
Paper from
responsible sources
FSC® C104740

Wayland is a division of
Hachette Children's Books,
an Hachette UK company.
www.hachette.co.uk

LIGHT?

Written by
KAY BARNHAM

Illustrated by
MIKE GORDON

WAYLAND

'Goodnight, Ruby!' said Mum, switching off
the bedside lamp. 'Sleep well.'
'Goodnight,' said Ruby.

The bedroom door closed.
Now, the only light came from the streetlight outside. Ruby looked at the book on her bedside table. She wished she could read a few more pages, but it was far too dark to see anything properly. Or was it ...?

'Aha!' said Ruby, remembering what was under her bed. She reached down and found what she was looking for.

Click! Ruby switched on the torch
and blinked in the sudden brightness.
'Now I can read my book,' she whispered, smiling.

'What is light?' asked Ruby the next morning.
'It's a type of energy,' explained Mum.
'It's because of light that we can see things.'

'What about the dark?' said Ruby, puzzled.
'Is that a type of energy too?'
Mum shook her head. 'When it's dark,
it just means that there's no light,' she said.

Mum, Ruby and her brother Oliver walked
to school. The sun shone brightly.
'Mum,' said Ruby curiously, 'why do
I have a shadow?'

'It's because you're blocking the sun's light,'
said Mum. 'It can't shine through you.'
'Look at my shadow puppets!' said Oliver,
making shapes with his hands.

That weekend, Mum, Ruby and Oliver went camping. They put up the tent. Then they spent the day at the beach. The sun shone brightly and the sea sparkled.

'The sun gives us lots of light, doesn't it?'
said Ruby, as they paddled.
'It's a light source,' said Mum, nodding.
'In fact, it's our biggest natural source of light.'

At sunset, streaks of red
and orange lit up the sky.
'What's that?' whispered Oliver.
He pointed to a tiny, yellow light
that bobbed about in the air.

'It's a firefly...' murmured Mum.
'How beautiful!'
'Awesome!' said Ruby. 'I didn't
know that an insect could be
a light source too.'

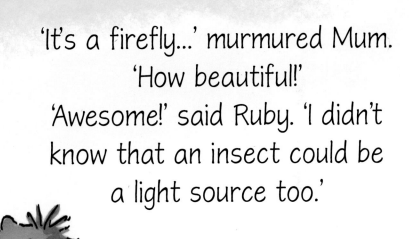

When it grew late, Mum lit a campfire.
Ruby and Oliver watched the flickering
flames as they toasted marshmallows.
Suddenly, Ruby grinned.
'Fire is another light source!' she said.
'Very good,' said Mum.

Oliver remembered
a huge storm.
'Lightning is another
light source!' he said.
'It's very bright and I wasn't
scared of it at all.'

Ruby switched on her torch. She watched
as its beam sliced through the darkness.
'That's artificial light,' said Mum. 'The light bulb
in your torch is made by humans and it's powered
by electricity. It doesn't just happen, like sunlight.'

'Do bedside lamps and streetlights make artificial light too?' asked Ruby. Mum smiled. 'Exactly!'

Stars twinkled in the inky sky.
'Look!' said Oliver, with a yawn. 'Starlight!'
'Well spotted,' said Mum. 'Stars are
another source of light.'

'Each star is actually a faraway sun ...' Ruby said thoughtfully. 'Starlight looks dim from Earth. But up close a star is very bright!'

A little later, the moon rose. It glowed in the starry sky. 'It's a full moon tonight,' said Ruby. 'The moonlight is so bright, I don't need my torch now!'

'The moon is different to other light sources,' said Mum. 'It doesn't make light. The moon reflects light from the sun.' 'Zzz ...' snored Oliver.

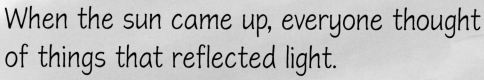

When the sun came up, everyone thought
of things that reflected light.
'The sea reflects sunlight,' said Ruby.
'See how it sparkles!'

'Glass reflects light too!' said Mum.
'So does a mirror!' said Ruby.
'And tin foil!' said Mum.
'And anything else smooth and shiny!'
added Oliver.

On the way home, they talked about how different light sources produced different amounts of light. 'Fireflies make hardly any light at all,' said Oliver.

26

'But the sun makes enough light
to illuminate the world,' said Ruby.
'The sun is so bright that you must never
look straight at it,' Mum reminded them.
'It would hurt your eyes.'

By the time they got home, it was dark.
'Let's go to the park,' said Mum mysteriously.
'There's one more kind of light that I'd like
to show you.'

Soon, the sky was filled with whooshes and whizzes
and pops and bangs and lots and lots of light.
'Fireworks!' cried Oliver.
'Awesome,' sighed Ruby.

NOTES FOR PARENTS AND TEACHERS

The aim of this book is to introduce children to scientific concepts in an entertaining, informative way. Here are some ideas for activities that will encourage them to think further about light and dark – and have fun doing it!

ACTIVITIES

1. Make a lisl of all the different light sources in this book.
Add any more light sources that you can think of. Now put them in order of brightness, from dimmest glow to most dazzling light!

2. One evening, switch off all the lights for one hour.
Now describe what it feels like. What can you see?

3 Can you rearrange these anagrams
to find five phrases to do with light and dark?

REF SKI ROW

I LIT AFRICA

HERBS STING

SEND ARKS

NAIL IT MULE

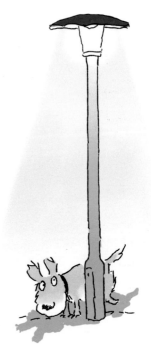

FIREWORKS, ARTIFICIAL, BRIGHTNESS,
DARKNESS, ILLUMINATE

SHADOW EXPERIMENT

Find a small window. On a sunny day, hold different materials up to the light. Try wood, cardboard, tissue paper, fabric, cling film or anything else you can find.

Make a list of which materials block light to make a solid shadow. These are opaque.

Which materials block a small amount of light and make a faint shadow? These are translucent.

Which materials block no light and make no shadow? These are transparent.

DID YOU KNOW ...?

Light is the fastest thing ever! It travels at nearly 300 million metres per second. It takes 8 minutes and 20 seconds for sunlight to travel from the Sun to Earth.

A solar eclipse happens when the Moon is between the Sun and the Earth. The Moon blocks the Sun's light, making a shadow on Earth. In a total eclipse, it becomes as dark as night.

BOOKS TO SHARE

Light and Dark
(*Ways into Science*)
by Peter Riley
(Watts Publishing, 2016)

Light
(*Amazing Science*)
by Sally Hewitt
(Wayland, 2014)

Light
(*Boom Science* series)
by Georgia Amson-Bradshaw
(Wayland, 2018)

Light
(*Fact Cat* series)
by Izzi Powell
(Wayland, 2018)

Light
(*How Does Science Work*)
by Carol Ballard
(Wayland, 2014)